Weeping for the Lovely Phantoms

JO COLLEY has compensated for a rootless childhood by living in the north east of England for the last thirty years. A prose writer and poet, she has read her work and spoken word performance pieces in the north east, Liverpool, London and Finland. Her work has been published by Vane Women, Sand and Ek Zuban, and she has been translated into Finnish. In 2007, she received a Northern Promise Award from New Writing North. She has a day job as a content developer for educational software.

Weeping for the Lovely Phantoms

Jo Colley

SALT

CAMBRIDGE

PUBLISHED BY SALT PUBLISHING
PO Box 937, Great Wilbraham, Cambridge CB21 5JX United Kingdom

© Jo Colley, 2007

First published 2007

Printed and bound in the United Kingdom by Biddles Ltd, King's Lynn, Norfolk

Typeset in Swift 9.5 / 13

ISBN 978 1 84471 305 9 hardback

Salt Publishing Ltd gratefully acknowledges
the financial assistance of Arts Council England

1 3 5 7 9 8 6 4 2

*"No more to say and nothing to weep for but the Beings in the Dream
trapped in its disappearance."*

from *Kaddish* ALLEN GINSBERG 1959

Contents

Acknowledgements

Some of the poems have appeared in the following magazines and publications: "Haig Street," *The Flesh of the Bear* (Ek Zuban 2004); "The Miss Havisham Papers 1," *Dreamcatcher* 2006; "Seven ways to leave your Lover," *Sand* 2005; "Accordion Player in Helsinki Harbour," *Other Poetry* 2007.

The author would like to acknowledge the financial support of a New Writing North Promise Award and of the Cultural Sector Development Initiative. I would like to thank Kate Fox, Jackie Litherland, Paul Summers and Andy Willoughby, for their support and advice. Special thanks to Angel Readman for her careful, critical eye.

Transformations

Dream on

As if our intricate labyrinthine code
could be deciphered through an hour long perusal
of the net curtain hung in your window
its Lancastrian rose motif repeated
over and over.

Snow White Rose Red
Don't beat your lover dead

Sometimes her image does not appear in the mirror.
She loses face—in fact
she practically gives it away,
photosynthesises in the dark
like a mushroom.
Purity is easy through willed disappearance.
She melts beside the fire
she builds for others.

Snow White Rose Red
Don't lie down upon his bed

Late evening sun ignites the nets
recasts the scene in a warm synthetic glow.
A rose is a cunt is a rose
flushed with exposure.
It's not that she enjoys humiliation:
her nature binds her to it
like a briar winds around a trellis.

Snow White Rose Red
Remember everything he said

In the cave everything and nothing makes sense.
The duality paralyses
cancels her out.
She's striped like a barber's pole
strobed unconscious
anaesthetised.

There aren't enough kisses in the world
to morph the bear
even though you could have sworn
you saw a glint of gold
beneath his rough exterior.

Snow White Rose Red
You'll never get inside his head

It was just a trick of the light.
Tiptoe past him on your way out.
Leave him to his long winter sleep.

Boro Girl

At the top of the steps outside the station
she's standing in her own winter zone
a cold blond, thin as a whip.
Her faraway eyes water
while the wind makes her bones reeds
that hum like the pipes of a forgotten tribe
lost somewhere on the Mongolian plains
eternally wandering.

An invisible blizzard swirls around her.
Caught in the snow queen's spell
the crystal carried in her veins
lodges in her heart
freeze frames her future.

She holds a bunch of tulips.
Her arms bend under their weight.
They are the colour of deoxygenated blood
the colour of the burst veins
on her skin's surface
the colour of the robe worn
by a Mongolian princess
on the day of her wedding.

Snow Patrol

I'm stuck in a snow drift.
Cotton wool flakes
fall faster than you can count them.
The sky is heavy, a goose feather quilt
emptying.

He happens by. Nice sledge—
Canadian built—and the dogs look fresh.
Their breath mingles with the steam
rising from their urgent bodies.

He's wearing dark glasses
but I can tell he's looking at me
He offers me the ride of my life.

I hop on, leave the car behind,
break the cardinal stay with your vehicle rule
like a woman with nothing to lose.

Before long the linen landscape
billows past.
I feel the stare behind the shades.
He states, "You're not from round here."
"No," I confirm, tongue unfreezing
from the roof of my mouth.

Satisfied, he yells at the dogs.
The sledge slips across the snow
makes a sound like a butcher's knife
drawn through flesh. Clean.

The arterial trees part to welcome us.
He throws a skin over my knees.
I'm warm, except for my hands.
Gloves are things I always lose
at least one of.
I reach under the skin, see it's bear
thick and brown, rough to the touch.

The bleached land melts into monochrome
as night unfolds.
We sledge on right through the night
stars replacing snow.

Goldilocks

This bed is too clean for the sex to be good.
The fabric is softened, scented with chemical flowers,
stains obliterated without trace.
A fresh sheet
like a virgin
every time you lie down.

This bed is too dirty to take your clothes off.
Hazardous substances lurk.
There's a biological odour —
X marks the spot of his latest conquest,
probably himself.

I'm looking for a bed that's just right.
Clean, but with a male smell,
a hint of testosterone that promises more
neither too hard nor disappointingly soft.
A bed that accommodates
then lets you go.

Remembering Lindisfarne

Rock pool eyes deep with secrets
the frilled seaweed's languid sway.
Beneath the smooth white sand
little crabs hide their soft bodies,
transparent fish show their workings,
ticking like tiny bombs.

The day her mother shut her out,
couldn't bear the sight of her:
a small girl with a ruined petticoat,
her face wet with tears in the tidy garden.
Innocent as sunlight
she learns about original sin,
doing time in the house of her mother's regret.

Her small starfish hands
cover the secrets in her pocket
wrapped in the white hanky
she can never be without.

When the sea eagle lifts her
gentle with his giant claws
she is not surprised.
He shows her the view
from the top of the cliffs,
the line drawn on the horizon.

Now her eyes hold
sea and sky.

Reprieve

The evening sky carbonates
a wedge of lemon
fizzes on the horizon
as the sun goes down.

A faint breeze disturbs the net curtains.
I'm sitting on the edge of your bed
in my underwear
elbows on my knees
like Edward Hopper's wife
playing herself for the umpteenth time
or an undercover cop
flat chested and ill at ease
working on an entrapment.

You are twitching, at your most canine
knowing
whatever you say will be taken down.
The glint of your teeth frames
your wet pink silent tongue.

You take the fifth.

I shut my face up in the martyr's hood
as if tranquilly accepting my fate
but the resentment hums in the room
like a wasp caught in a jar.
A modern jazz quartet improvise
around a theme of miscues
cacophonies the silence.

Then the light changes. A shift
in the atmosphere as if a storm passed.
You assume your shape, turn
from dog to man, reach out for me

with words. Their power melts
my resistance.

Your hands undo me.

Kabuki noh

I sit beside you in the sushi bar
my friend of thirty years or even more
your face to me unchanged, immune to time
but causing you to mourn the way we fade.
The mirrored walls,
the tables, lacquered black to a hard shine,
repeat our images around the room.
We are not young. We were never perfect
like the girl who sits behind you
geisha like, among a group of men
who wield chopsticks like samurai
competing for her smile.

In the Ladies we confront the mirror
pull back our skin, stretch it tight
transform to Kabuki masks, stern and held,
look for possibilities of nip and tuck
laugh and break the mould.

Hansel and Gretel and the Sugar Rush Granny

She lures them to the sugar house
the pick and mix treasury
the select and suck
choose and chew
magic that is taboo.

She shows them where the coconut mushrooms grow
traces the path of the sherbet sputniks
binds them with liquorice shoelaces
lets the colours of the e-numbers
dance a rainbow in their blood
until they are weak and twitching and sick.

Then they are hers:
drowsing under the duvet
in front of the television
their eyes glazed like humbugs
their breath sour
their teeth assaulted
their minds lulled into quiet.

They can't find their way home
having lost interest in breadcrumbs
unable to distinguish
the neutral shades of pebbles.

Absentmindedly she pinches their thighs
their upper arms

just testing.

Seven Ways to Leave Your Lover

1. Slowly and painfully—tied
    to the wheel like St Catherine
    rolling down the years
    until at 360° you find yourself
    upright enough to see straight.
    Untie yourself.
    Crawl away.

2. Accidentally—you get on
    the wrong train
    travel miles in another direction.
    Scanning the scenery for something familiar
    realise you like the new view.
    Get off
    at the next stop.

3. Amicably—you have worn together
    like a foot in a shoe
    comfortable—except you are the shoe
    downtrodden and near enough worn out.
    You slip off
    leg it.
    You're miles away before he notices.

4. Earnestly—with the help
    of specialists, in a room
    with bad paintings of the Lake District
    a box of tissues on the table.
    Money changes hands.
    You kiss on both cheeks
    leave in separate cars.

5. Acrimoniously—china is thrown
   against walls you painted
   doors are kicked, wood splinters, glass shatters
   recriminations hover in the air
   like hornets released from confinement.
   You run for safety.
   Seek asylum.

6. Secretly—after years of planning
   wearing a disguise, you have
   leaked dreams from your pockets
   kicked over the traces
   until nothing is left.
   You are repatriated.
   No one remembers you.

7. Finally—the car will not
   turn into that road again
   your feet must be retrained
   to avoid that path
   your arms to resist
   the urge to hold him
   your eyes, knowing about salt,
   must never look back.

Moving Image

Hitchcock Blonde

Ice cool.
A frosted Barbie
hard and cold to the touch
her hour glass figure
infinitely breakable.

Examine her carefully.
The painted blue eyes
with built in tears
(press button A)
the immaculate underwear
uneasily prised
from her brittle carapace.

Shoe her in black
lay a tailored suit
on a firm foundation
restrain the breasts
(remove nipples first)
contain the ample derriere.

But still she will run
shackled for our entertainment
hobble to the nearest lake
the highest tower
fling herself in
or off.

Drama queen.

Torture her
against a backdrop of nuns
an op art chorus line.
She will raise a tiny hand
gloved in pearl grey.
Listen.
"Scotty," she will murmur.
"Don't let me go."

Marnie

The brisk click clack of her heels
on the sidewalk
as she walks away with the contents of the safe
cached in her calfskin case.

Her new hair glistens above the collar
of her tailored suit
dark glasses tone down
the gleam of triumph in her guarded eyes.

It's the best moment:
getting away with it—the cash
an incidental bonus
a side effect she disperses
fast as she can.

The art of her face, a blank canvas
she remakes with layers of paint
using identikit transfers as a guide
a mistress of disguise.

A perfect life.
Horses, clothes and luggage.

If she could only ditch that mother,
lurking in the background in a cardboard house
the intermittent morse of a tapped stick
spirit rap
dragging her back.

The Bodega Bay Incident

The line of her suit is the line of the coast
is the line of her Aston Martin.
Its convertible curves cruise into Bodega Bay
insinuate her into the scene.
She's a Bunty cutout with no vpl
stuck on a canvas of a sixties seaside print:
a washed out beach, some grass,
gulls flying against a melodramatic sky.

It's quiet. No-one about.
Everyone is waiting for her to start the story,
promenade across the page
make it turn
like Pandora opening the box.
Meanwhile the townsfolk linger in wardrobe
uneasy
awaiting their cue.

And the birds.
The birds gather like clouds
emit high frequency signals
received on the skin.
They have grievances, old wounds,
a history of foul play.

The silence is deafening.
Oblivious, she stalks her mate,
while the sun glints on her elegant coiffure,
coiled like a giant snail, inviting.

He kisses the back of her neck
marks the spot
where the birds will strike.
And they do.

In a beautiful sunset she is carried away
bleeding like St Sebastian from many wounds
her lovely flesh pierced and ravaged.
Her eyes stare blindly from their sockets
while the black-capped crows look on devoutly.
Sentence has been carried out.

Shadows

Uncle Charlie has a secret
he wants me to share
"Just you and me," he says
because I'm special.

Up the Hitchcock stairs with Uncle Charlie
to the room where the sunlight
casts busy shadows on the walls.
While he shows his secret

I watch the patterns change
listen to a blackbird ask a question
the wind search the trees.

On the landing all the doors are shut
There's no knowing what you'll find
on the other side.

Down the Hitchcock stairs with Uncle Charlie.
He hums a little tune
one big hand on the banister
the other on my shoulder.

In the kitchen mother wipes her hands
on her baking apron.
There's cake with cherries on for tea.

Bates Motel

Because it is raining and she is tired.
The weight of her secret oppresses her:
through the windscreen wipers' blur
the colours and lights run
like mascara on a tearstained face.
She wants definition
checks into the Bates Motel
a place to reconsider.
Restructure.
Redo her make up.
Return.
But first she needs a shower.

Welcome to the Hotel Caledonia

There's a view that stretches to infinity
via parallel lines: the river beaded with light
the road back to the city
a darkening horizon shafted by highrise.

Architectural gems grace the towpath:
an armadillo crouches hoarding sound
a hatchery of offices glow in vacant confidence
spawn robot office staff within.

The Clyde quivers in the chill night breeze
looks troubled. Elderly.
Weary with its transformation
nipped and tucked beyond endurance
mutton dressed as sushi.

It's a Ridley Scott homage
shot with film noir
everything in black and white
except those lights, a north sea legacy
leaking sulphur
bleeding propane.

From the sixth floor of the Hotel Caledonia
you see the taxi make its slow approach.
The way the headlamps swing in your direction
seek you out like tracker dogs
lungs bursting with the scent of your discarded skin.

The taxi pulls up, leaves its engine running.
Three of them get out.
You can tell by the way
they shake their trouser legs
adjust their crombies
they're packing hardware.

It's a no win. A done deal.
With nowhere left to run
you sit on one of the twin beds
your back to the door.
Wait for the terse knock
the questions you can't answer.
Dread the moment when
they force your pillowcased head
under the water for the final time.

Homemade dress

The girl in the home made dress
knows Jesus loves her.
It's written in the big book
her name, Norma Jean.
She'll be coming home to glory
one day.

The black and white dog
who runs beside her
loves her too—his pink tongue
administers wet kisses until
the next door neighbour
shoots him dead.

Accordion Player in Helsinki Harbour

The tune tumbles over the harbour
in nostalgic waves, recalling a past
you had no part in but somehow feel you lived –
the hardship of the war years, hoarding
food in the dacha, looking for mushrooms
in dew wet fields at dawn
the last of the dried reindeer stowed
in the innermost babuschka
saved for the youngest child
a soldier's cap, clutched in an old woman's hand,
snow covered boots dripping by the door
cross stitched hearts hung over the stove
commemorate a homecoming

it's as though the trees have whispered
from their split bark mouths
an archive implanted like a chip of ice
deep in the Baltic of memory
slowly dissolving in the blood.

Still Lives

Rowing on Derwent Water

November. A pewter sky
lids the wrinkled lake.
We are alone on Derwent Water
out of season
stuck with a stygian bargain
we struck
in another world.

I take the oars, feel
my fingers blister as the prow
slits the waves
keep an even keel
as you stand up, mid water
a dark silhouette
like the cormorants perched on the rocks
ink marks on the grey canvas of the lake.

The fragile craft bobs.
My heart lurches as a seagull
sings in high lonesome overhead.
Your face is empty.

Later my mother tells
how she rowed my father on the same lake
sixty years ago
one perfect May morning on their honeymoon.
Her land army shoulders powered him across
as he sat in the stern, a bundle of bones
reclaimed from the POW camp.

Picture them. Her full red mouth
thick dark hair.
She is blooming in a forties print, while he
watches her, half his fighting weight
plotting a comeback.

Cherry Picker

He can't sleep for thinking of them — hanging
dark red, in fleshy clusters
their tight moonlit skins shine
bright enough for birds to see their faces in.

Then when he sleeps, he dreams
lithe lads sit astride the branches
shake down a heavy crimson rain
to village girls stood beneath the trees
their aprons spread.

At dawn he leaves the house
fruit machine eyes spinning.
He's gone for hours
comes home laden
stained purple
sated.

Things He Knows

Logs. Their whereabouts and burnability.
How to merge with the woods
gimlet eyes probing for the fallen.
How to hack them with your axe
pile them up like corpses
return under cover of darkness
and spirit them away.

Fires. How to build one
with the lonely hearts page from the Echo
loosely crumpled like lost knickers
some twigs and the first log
chosen for size, dryness and shape
applied at the right moment
to catch the spark.

Fungus. The lethal and the sweet.
How to find them, hidden in the grass
or under autumn trees.
How to lift their skirts to check
the colour of their petticoats
test with your tongue
decide.

Spiders. Where they live
inside and out. How to
entice them from their hidden lairs
by a gentle tapping on a dry stone wall
the flurry as they emerge
looking for prey
their disappointed slow retreat.

Haig Street

In the car outside your house
waiting for you,
watch the sun chase shadows down the street
like a hot flush
leaving the pavements
drenched in light.
Pigeons circle surveillance overhead:
where's the fire?
Nothing moving in this neighbourhood.

Behind boarded up facades
banged up couples in
Fred Perry and tracky bottoms
smoke L & B and blow
watch Sky TV
text big brother
while the kids play out, make mosaic
out of broken glass and old lottery tickets
experiment in the stolen caravan
a wendy house of dreams in never never land.

Shostakovic on the car radio.
Remember the Lenin museum in Tampere?
The man with the visionary beard
could never have pictured this.
Up the street the wind blows fireweed seeds
from overgrown allotments.
The workers sit in their condemned houses
like Indians on the reservation
turning the beads over and over in their empty hands.

The Miss Havisham Papers

1. WEDDING DAY

Hope and disappointment balance the scales:
the result is a tranquil zero.

I rise early, bathe my face in dew
look out on a May morning
put on my dress for you.

Life begins and ends on the same day.

In the churchyard my white dress flutters
like a flag of surrender
clouds freeze in the sky.
I am a stone angel
rooted to my witness spot
transfixed.

The cake is a white tower
reaching to heaven
damask dazzles
I am snowblind
mummified in satin rags.

I place a ringless hand on the table
begin my zombie walk
learn to live with absence
like the loss of a limb.

After a while white becomes sepia
a forgotten photograph
found in the drawer of a new house.
The tatters of my satin dress trail behind me.
My skin has dried to faded rose petals.

One tear each year
a slow stalactite
suspended over my life
a cold crystal dagger
waiting for you.

I rise early
look out over a May morning
see you ride over the fields.
Remember your blue eyes
the warmth of your hand.

2. MISS HAVISHAM AND THE ROSES

Cliché: to mark our anniversary
you send a dozen roses, velvet red,
a message written by your secretary
no doubt concocted in some hotel bed.
Each complex heart is hothoused into life
protected from the weather, fragrance free
the kind of flowers you order for your wife
to offset random infidelity.
They never bloom or rot, but fade away
like paper flowers bleaching in the light.
Their slick perfection suits our special day
their sexless emblematic cool seems right.
A bead of dew poised on a glossy leaf:
my tongue tastes salt, my foolish heart relief.

3. Miss Havisham in the Garden

Out of the blue, the clear sky darkened.
A wind from nowhere shook the anxious trees
I stood beside the trellis in the garden
still as a statue in the gathering breeze
my fingers round the neck of a dying rose.
As the air stirred the summer trees
the leaves whispered
with the voices of missing children.

Thunder roamed the sky, restless,
unappeased, and in the pauses
angry lightning flashed.
I waited for the rain
but only a few drops fell.

Diversification

His mother was a cow.
Hadn't a bean to leave him
after she'd drunk herself to death
on the compo from the foot and mouth.

But still, he mourned her, in his way,
mixed her ashes with John Innes
watered in each seed with his tears.

Under the false ceiling in the old barn
the indoor hens bask, bird flu free,
quiet as doves. They fluff their feathers
in the rays of the metal arc,
leaking through the floorboards,
lay like angels, always a brown egg.

He's not worried. Doesn't know
how long before they work it out.
Doesn't care. In his dreams
he dives into a warm sea
swims until his limbs feel free.

From the long field, he looks back
to the house, its lighted windows.
Lets the smoke of his joint drift
under the big night sky.

The Woman Who Became a Sofa

At first I could make it to the store
pick up supplies, check out the offers
hurry back with my paper sack
bulging with goodies.
Then, for a while, I was still able
to hit the kitchen
fry a sandwich, microwave a burger
unbox a pie.
Over the years, movement became a struggle
I couldn't get up the momentum
the interest.
But a girl's got to eat so I called in the welfare.
They helped me access the food source
fed me like Jumbo in the zoo
a bag of buns on the hour
a bucket of coke
super size fries.

In time I became the sofa.
My body fluids soaked the polystyrene:
the microfibres met mine and merged,
a lingering mystery, like a marriage.
Look at me now and wonder:
my cushion breasts
plush dimpled arms
the gentle sigh as you lower yourself
into the welcome sink of my lap.
I no longer need feeding
just a dust with a damp cloth
a little plumping
to accentuate my best features.

Cornflowers in a Pot

Six of them, thin stemmed soldiers
evenly spaced, with leaves
that start out straight
then droop a little sadly.

The flower heads
angled like table lamps
tight as fists
waiting for something
to make them open
turn them on.

Star Gazing

Why did we choose that night, after years of idle talk
to go out in search of meteorites? The line between us
worn so thin, I was hanging by a thread
above the void, suspended.

In the darkest spot we could find
we opened the sun roof, lay back
with our binoculars, swept the sky
like snipers, checking for movement.

Whilst we argued about time zones,
the names of constellations, which way is up,
the sky slyly drew a soft grey veil
over her sequinned nakedness

deeming us unworthy to behold
the Leonides in flight. For a while
we scrutinised each cloud tear
longing for a glimpse, a flash, a spark.

Nothing but emptiness.
I drove you home,
returned to my cold house
falling, falling until I hit the earth.

Landscape of Argument

Always a road and a car
Or a room and a bed
Or a street and a pub

Always a turned back
A tapping foot
Something broken

Always a phonecall
Intermittent signal
Traffic passing

Sometimes a silence
Stones in our mouths
Lips stitched

Sometimes words rumble
Thunder coming
Or an avalanche

This time nothing
Lunar wastes
Craters.

East of England

Trent. Ouse. Nene. Yare.
The monosyllabic rivers of England
follow their unromantic course
through the eastern flatlands
accidentally spelling your name.

No-one has told them the world is round
or that ordinary decent people
can be diverted into murky waters
to which they return in dreams.

The rivers begin at source, come out in the Wash.
What happens after that is not their concern.
Enough to flow, deep green, secret
under the quiet trees.

Beautiful People

In August, 1969, five people were murdered in a house on Cielo Drive in Beverly Hills California, by members of Charles Manson's sect, known as The Family.

CAST

SHARON TATE: film actress, wife of Roman Polanski, eight months pregnant with his child

ROMAN POLANSKI: Polish film director, husband of Sharon, absent at the time of her murder.As a child during WW2, he spent time in the Kracow ghetto, where he saw his mother taken by the Nazis. She subsequently died in Auschwitz.

JAY SEBRING: well known Californian hair stylist, who styled the hair of many famous people of the time including Jim Morrison of The Doors. Sharon's ex-boyfriend.

ABIGAIL VOLGER: heiress to a fortune made in coffee, wealthy socialite who had dabbled in social work and civil rights

WOJCIECH FRYKOWSKI: Polish actor, friend of Polanski's and Abigail Volger's boyfriend

CHARLES MANSON: leader of the sect known as The Family, still serving a prison sentence for his part in a spate of murders in late 60s California, although he was not at the scene of the Sharon Tate murders

SUSAN ATKINS: member of the Family, still in prison for the Tate murders

PATRICIA KRENWINKLE: member of the Family, still in prison for the Tate murders

CHARLES "TEX" WATSON: member of The Family, still in prison for the Tate and LaBianca murders

LINDA KASABIAN: member of the Family who received immunity from prosecution for the Tate murders for testifying before a Grand Jury

Weightless

Those last days—the heat of August
like a hot soup she swims in
sleep sipped like a cool drink
through the thick curtained nights.

The child rides her from inside
his heels kickstarting her
long before dawn. Demanding
like his father: but contained.

He tenants her.
Her celluloid flesh takes shape
around this ordinary miracle
like a carved Madonna.

Through the stilled days
she floats in the pool,
weightless. An undiscovered planet
orbiting in liquid space.

Forget the man you love.
Let him fade from your mind
like the memory of your waistline
his careless infidelities

like a dog fucking on your perfect
sprinklered lawn. Forget
those hands, the tender cruelty
he brought to your bed

before he left, to conquer
new worlds, plant the adopted flag
a moonwalker secure in
his impenetrable suit.

Let him go. The long day
moves towards its close.
Crickets start to sing as
the heat gives its final gasp.

It's time to go inside,

Homecoming Queen

Miss Tiny Tot of Dallas
sunny smiles her way
into the hearts of the soldiers
lined up outside her doll's house.

Grows into Sharon Marie
learns to button up her nightie
when daddy's home.

Ripens into a perfect peach
you want to sink your teeth in.

On the platform, one hip tilted forward
the bright coloured sash
displays her like a new fridge:
Miss Richland Washington
Miss Autorama
Homecoming queen.

Make it a Real Nice Murder

Charlie checks them over
the girls and Tex, sends them
over the hill on their first mission
over the edge of the helter skelter
no going back.
They are his barefoot soldiers
his Vietcong spiked with methedrine
a distant twister coming up fast
through the peachy Californian dusk.

It's a fine August night
ripe for pig killing.
The air is soft as velvet.
On Cielo Drive the fairy lights sparkle
around the homes of the rich
their unassailable lives.

"Leave a sign," Charlie tells them
as the old yellow Ford
winds its way to the top of the hill.
"You know. Something witchy."

Great Looking Chicks

Charlie's here with all these great looking chicks!
He plays the guitar and he's a real wild guy.
He has all these girls hanging out like servants.
You can come over and just fuck any of them you want!

Lipstick Traces

Lipsticks I stole from my mother's handbag
buried under Kensitas and Chanel No 5
the shiny cases like the bullets we uncovered
in the woods around the camp
dusted with powder from her leaking compact.
Passionate Red
Tangerine Twist
Coral Kiss

Factor to the Max

She feels the pressure of their CAT scan eyes
the boys who press against her in recess
undressing her to the bone.

They need to feel the glow of her
a girl so golden she radiates light
from her toes to the plump curls
that tumble to her sculpted shoulders.

She hears their smutty mutterings
but stays quiet, entraps them in her level gaze
appraises them zit by zit.

They slink off like dogs, uncertain, shamed.
She wonders what they want.
Their wet mouths. The look in their eyes.

6os Wedding

Why not? It's just a piece of paper.
Decide in a split second
before the moment goes
fix it up before you change your mind.

His stag night—the swinging London club
nameless starlets glimmer in the dark
scattered amongst celebrities like candy
his sweet tooth is powerless to resist.

The morning after
he wears a green velvet suit
to match his skin
lace at his neck like a flunky
more frog than prince.

Her wedding dress stops
the traffic in the King's Road
so mini it's minus.
Her legs stretch to infinity
Pearl buttons stud the cuffs.
Flowers and ribbons in her hair.

Jay Sebring

Half a lifetime spent coiffing the rich
in the heat and din of the salon
your hands itchy with chemicals
as you run them through their expensive dos.

(Those hippy chicks—nothing
on their locks, just washed
then left to hang, refusing
to be styled. Who could
make a living out of them?)

Sharon's hair is beautiful.
Soft and pliant in your fingers
the molten strands wind around the rollers
good as gold.

Her face in the mirror as she looks at you.
Perfect symmetry of her American bones.
She gives you her high school smile

gives you her high school ring.
It's still on your finger when the LAPD
find you. Shot, stabbed and kicked to death.
Your hair stiff with blood.

Beautiful People

The boys on the California beach
throw their American bodies onto the surf
let it scrub them clean like a mother
scouring their ears with salt.

The long limbed girls cook
lightly dressed in bikinis
basted with Ambre Solaire.

These are the lucky ones
Orange County perfect
blind as mannequins gazing through opaque glass
believing they're safe.

Abigail Folger

Poor little rich girl
no side-stepping your inherited life
aromatic with privilege
bitter with taboo.

Walk the line in your Catholic school
experiment with social work
find it impossible to face
the way most people live.

Try acid and mda
to break you open.
Sleep with a man you know will stay
because you pay.

In the warm chemical glow
you fail to recognise
the smiling face of murder
the deadly barefoot girls.

The last ditch fight
to preserve your life
your finest hour.
You make it hard for them

go to your death
in a white nightdress
splattered with blood
like a virgin bride.

Romanson

In the grey ruined city of Cracow
Behind the walls of the ghetto
Where the dead lie in the streets
He learns to live.
He was a child
Saw his mother dragged away
Loaded on the back of a truck

a trailer park
hidden from the rich
like trash nobody wants
He learns his worth
before he learns to talk
he's traded for a pint of beer

He watched her leave.
She did not smile or wave
Just looked at him
He spent a lifetime
replaying the scene.

His mother had no use for him.
her blurred face

in his inner room

I couldn't look at you son.
It wasn't easy but I knew
I had to turn my back
Your life is more important.
Live and remember me.

You looked like the devil.
I had to leave you
before you took my soul
You're better off without me.

She never came back.
He never lost the pain.
Punished every woman he met
For not being her.

He gave up waiting.
Internalised the ache
made them pay
Made them his children

Taught them the meaning of pain
Until he learned
The pain is his
No matter how he tries
To pass it on.

the swift slide into chaos
baptism by blood and fire
there is no limit
he can never fail

Charlie's Angel 1: Susan Atkins

She didn't want to die, said Susan, laughing.
You should have heard her beg.
She thought because she was pregnant
she was safe.

No way. I told her straight.
Listen bitch, I said. You're gonna die.
I don't care about you.
I don't feel anything at all.

After we killed her, I licked the blood from my hands.
I would have cut out the baby as a present for Charlie
but there wasn't time.
He would have liked that.
What a trip that would have been.

Charlie's Angel 2: Patricia Krenwinkle

Patricia loves Jesus, collects
the pretty cards on Sundays
admires the bruises blooming
on her schoolgirl knees
at prayer before the mirror
in her LA bedroom.

Enraptured, she dreams.
She will take the veil, make vows
that bind her to a life of quiet contemplation.
She will dwell in a simple cell
Christ's devoted bride.

But later, when the world turns
psychedelic, bright colours burn through
her closed eyelids, form
a different vision.
A new Messiah
blinds her with his laser stare
offers revelation with a pill.

From there to here.
She stares into the bottomless pit
becomes a death angel
ribbons the flesh of the chosen
bathes herself in their blood.
A baptism.
A rebirth.

Full circle brings her to a single cell
a life spent in quiet contemplation.
Patricia helps those less fortunate to read
recites the alphabet whilst
the loop in her head plays over and over:
her reddened hand carves WAR in human flesh.

Charlie's Angel 3: Linda Kasabian

I didn't think she'd talk—but
that's the one thing she's good at
the one thing she's really famous for.

Let me take you down
Cos I'm going to

She was so pretty—that fresh face
long straight hair and perfect chin
blossoming innocence
an American flower, a Sharon twin
but without the breaks.

She hasn't aged so well,
uses still, and that can take its toll.

I read the news today—oh boy.

"Yeah, sure, I was there that night.
It was me that drove the car.
I didn't know what was happening.
We just did what Charlie said
slid down the helter skelter
because he told us to."

Living is easy with eyes closed

"He was so beautiful.
Special. His eyes could see inside you.
I wanted to do whatever he wanted."

There's nothing you can do that can't be done.

"But I couldn't kill anybody.
The screams.
The blood.
The way the man looked at me then passed."

See how they run like pigs from a gun.

"It was the longest night of my life.
I was pregnant at the time.
I think the nightmare echoed in my womb.
She's never been a happy child.
We live how we can, day to day.
Sometimes, I think
I'd be better off in prison."

It's getting hard to be someone . . .

She lights a cigarette and stares into the TV.
Her eyes see nothing.
I let myself out.

Wipe Out

Let's shave our heads, Susan says.
We'll show them we're not like them
They don't understand the process.
Let's do it for Charlie.

Their bald heads glow under the courtroom lights
like smooth white mushrooms
closed caps
forced in manure.
Their young faces stare out
blank as babies
Buddhist nuns afloat
on a sea of contemplation
plucking petals from the lotus
chemically cleansed.

That night intrudes in flashbacks.
Maybe they dreamt it.
Maybe it was someone else
who held the knife
held down the victims
like pigs at the slaughter
ignored the tears and pleas
washed off the blood in a freeway toilet
went home
to their own children.

Weeping for the Lovely Phantoms

1. NOWHERESVILLE

The muffled house releases me as Sunday
holds its breath. I slip beyond the town
to join the ceremony on the hill
where ash tree priests are waiting, robed and cauled
their whispered questions carried by the breeze.
They offer keys to unlock mysteries
direct me to the brook, where float
the pictures in my head I can't erase
or wash away. They stay, hard nuggets
in my throat, gag me til I speak his name.
It drifts up to the clouds, a lost balloon
that disappears from view as the bells
begin the call to evensong.

2. UNCLE TONY

He was the homely youngest son, the one
who stayed behind, nursed a dying mother
whilst the others flew off into their lives.
A genial giant, psychiatric nurse, good Christian
he brought us books that tried to teach us things:
How Big is Big? the concrete sixties facts
he thought we ought to know
the black and white of life.

On Sunday mornings, whilst the house
sleeps off the night before
I climb into his bed, take him
the fairy tales my father bought but never read
show him Cinderella, Snow White, Rose Red
whilst his big hands lift my nightie
tickle til it hurts.

3. GARDEN

Mum and I in the garden
digging up potatoes like grave robbers
everything a conspiracy.
She makes me throw heavy stones into the bucket
so Fred next door will think
we've brought forth monsters from our unruly patch
not disciplined like his.

Each forkload of earth
uncovers sweet small spheres
that disappoint her
but sit inside my hand
their loamy smell a comfort
like her scones in the oven
meat roasting
toast before the fire
the bedtimes stories
I refused to let her change
needing a happy ending.

4. FIREWEED

The rose bay willow herb shrills amethyst
in short sharp bursts. Then as summer's
deeper blue ascends, shreds and shifts
into soft white strands that float like airships
take flight
snag and catch in the leaves of other plants
each bearing a dark seed.

Herb Robert. The plant that bears his name.
Old man's beard that drifts into his season:
late September, signing autumn's start.
Your old man's beard on your old man's chest
the last hours as your child's eyes dimmed
to the slowing rhythm of your heart.

5. GREEN

A summer's morning lights me out of bed
over the fields to Dingle where the woods
bleed bluebells and the air is scented
as the bath cubes in my mother's drawer
the ones I gave her
that she never used.

The long stemmed grass reaches to my waist
snags in my straight brown hair, pulls me down
to hide in its secret world. The iridescent light
casts shadows which criss cross my skin
like a legacy of self harm.
The summer breeze moves the soft hairs on my arms
its faint chill stings my nose like smelling salts
opens a window in my head.
I stand and stride triumphant through the green,
sharp and clean
as a marguerite coming into flower

upside down on the horizon
a city's mirage waits.